## JOURNAL

Sta
End Date: __/__/____

This Journey belongs to:

# Still Waters

## A JOURNEY THROUGH
## LECTIO DIVINA

A DEVOTIONAL BY

## Samara Elledge

# Discovering Tranquility:

## A Journey Through Lectio Divina

*But when the Father sends the Advocate as my representative—that is, the Holy Spirit—he will teach you everything and will remind you of everything I have told you. - Jesus*
**John 14:26 NLT**

In the rush of modern life, where information inundates and demands for our attention seem ceaseless, the art of deep contemplation and quiet connection to our Creator often takes a backseat. It's in these moments of quiet introspection that practices like Lectio Divina emerge as guiding lights, illuminating a path to inner serenity, spiritual growth, and a deepened connection to the Holy Spirit. God desires an active relationship with us. Derived from ancient monastic traditions, Lectio Divina is not merely a Bible reading exercise, but a transformative journey that invites us to actively engage with the Scriptures in a profound and intimate way, guiding us in finding a personal message from and conversation with God.

At its heart, Lectio Divina is a four-step process that encourages us to approach Scripture with openness, mindfulness, and receptivity. The Latin term which translates to "divine reading" encapsulates a practice that invites us to read a chosen text multiple times, each time deepening our connection to its words and allowing the Holy Spirit to guide us in unfolding its layers of meaning. As we progress through the stages of Lectio (reading), Meditatio (reflection), Oratio (response), and Contemplatio (restful contemplation), we embark on a cyclical journey that nurtures not only our understanding of God's living word, but also our relationship with ourselves, the world, and Christ.

In this meditation journal, we embark on a personal expedition through the landscapes of our inner selves and our connection with God using the time-honored practice of Lectio Divina. Each page will be a canvas upon which you paint your thoughts, emotions, and insights as you engage with God's living word. As you embark on this journey, remember that there is no rush; the wisdom of Lectio Divina encourages us to dwell in the spaces between words, to savor the silences, and to listen to the Holy Spirit's guidance and allow the Scripture, which is alive, to help grow your relationship with God. May this journal be your companion, a vessel for your revelations, and a haven where the art of divine reading merges with the art of self-discovery and communion with the Lord.

♡ Samara

# An Intro to Lectio Divina & the purpose of this journal

We practice Lectio Divina intending to foster a deeper, more intimate connection with God while utilizing the Scriptures as our guiding companions in prayer. As we immerse ourselves in the profound wisdom of these Scriptures and find solace in moments of stillness, we create a sacred space where the Holy Spirit can gently unveil His presence and illuminate the path of divine purpose that awaits us. In the quietude of contemplation, we invite a profound encounter with God and a revelation of His unique design for our lives. Lectio Divina becomes the vessel through which we seek, listen, and commune with God, nurturing a relationship that transcends words and time.

## Lectio (Reading)

The first step of Lectio Divina sets the stage for a contemplative encounter with Scripture. As you read the chosen passage, approach it with an open heart and a receptive mind. Read the words out loud, slowly and attentively, allowing them to wash over you like ripples in a serene pond. In this phase, you're not seeking deep analysis or intellectual comprehension; instead, you're creating a space for the words to resonate within you. Read the passage three times, quietly or out loud. As you linger over each word and phrase, let them evoke feelings, memories, or thoughts without the pressure of immediately understanding their significance. Simply have faith that the Holy Spirit will speak to you through the words.

## Meditatio (Meditation)

Moving into the second phase, Meditatio, you transition from reading to reflecting. This step invites you to delve deeper into the words that captured your attention during the initial reading. Choose a word, phrase, or concept that speaks to you and write these down. Contemplate its layers of meaning. Allow your mind to wander, exploring connections between the chosen words and your life experiences. This is a moment of active engagement, where you might ask questions like: How does this resonate with my current journey? What emotions does it stir within me? What is God revealing to your heart through this text? Through such contemplation, you create a bridge between the Scriptures and your thoughts and emotions.

## Oratio (Response)

The third phase, Oratio, invites you to respond authentically to the insights that God has shown you during your meditation. This is a dialogue between yourself and God, a chance to express your gratitude, hopes, concerns, and intentions. Let your response become a heartfelt prayer, a journal entry, or a conversation with God. Your words need not be polished or perfect; what matters is the sincerity with which you communicate. Share your thoughts with God; tell Him what is on your heart, what is weighing you down, and what you are grateful for. Write out some or all of your prayer as you offer it to God. There are extra journaling pages throughout the journal should you need more space to write your prayers.

## Contemplatio (Contemplation)

In the final phase of Lectio Divina, Contemplatio, you enter a space of stillness and receptivity. This step mirrors the quiet moments of meditation, allowing the echoes of the reading, reflection, and response to settle within you as you rest in God's love. Instead of actively seeking answers or revelations, you surrender to the peace of simply being. This contemplative silence is akin to gazing at a landscape with awe, where you let go of the need to dissect and analyze. Instead, allow the beauty of the moment to envelop you. As you rest in this contemplative state, you open yourself to the possibility of receiving insights from the Holy Spirit that transcend the confines of logic and language.

Through these four interconnected phases of Lectio Divina, you embark on a profound journey of self-discovery, spiritual connection, and creative expression. This meditation journal invites you to embrace each step, integrating the wisdom of Scripture with the introspective art of meditative drawing, as you navigate deepening your relationship with God.

# How to use this Lectio Divina Journal

*"Blessed is the one who does not walk in step with the wicked or stand in the way that sinners take or sit in the company of mockers, but whose delight is in the law of the Lord, and who meditates on his law day and night. That person is like a tree planted by streams of water, which yields its fruit in season and whose leaf does not wither— whatever they do prospers."*
**Psalms 1:1-3 NIV**

The purpose of this journal is to help you connect daily with the Scriptures and the Holy Spirit. We hope that it will lead you to grow in your walk with God. Each day you select which Bible translation you would like to use for the daily reading. We've also added five elements to the Lectio process to help you with focus and tranquility: quietude, weekly examen prayer (solo or as a family), journaling, meditative art, and meaningful action.

## Quietude

We've added this simple step to help you prepare for each day's sacred reading with a few moments of quieting the mind and soul. Center yourself and you could even offer a short prayer to God asking Him to be with you while you enter His Word and to open your heart. Ask Him to lead, guide, and direct your path.

## Cultivating Presence: The Weekly Examen for Reflective Prayer

In the tapestry of our weekly journey through life, moments often pass by in a whirlwind, leaving behind traces of experiences, emotions, and encounters that shape our paths. The Weekly Examen, a cherished practice of reflective prayer, offers us a lantern to illuminate these fleeting moments and uncover the presence of the divine within them. Rooted in the Ignatian tradition, this practice guides us through a deliberate review of our week, helping us discern God's subtle guidance, recognize blessings, and become more attuned to the whispers of our hearts.

Once weekly you will find your Weekly Examen with prompts as well as room for journaling and reflection.

# Step 1: Gratitude for God's Presence

Begin your Weekly Examen by grounding yourself in the awareness of God's constant presence. Take a moment to close your eyes and breathe deeply, allowing your mind to settle. Inhale with gratitude for the week that has passed and exhale any tension or distractions. With each breath, acknowledge God as the source of your existence and the guiding force throughout your week. Cultivate a sense of gratitude for the gift of life and the opportunity to engage in this prayerful reflection.

# Step 2: Review of the Week

Slowly replay the events of your week in your mind's eye. Start from the beginning of the week and move chronologically through its activities and encounters. Notice both significant and seemingly insignificant moments: conversations, tasks, encounters, emotions, and reactions. As you review, observe your emotions, intentions, and how you felt connected or disconnected from your inner values during this week-long journey.

# Step 3: Recognition of God's Presence

In this step, seek moments where you distinctly felt the presence of the divine during the week. These could be instances of joy, inspiration, comfort, or a sense of guidance. They might emerge as encounters with nature, moments of genuine connection with others, or sudden insights that you attribute to the Holy Spirit. Embrace these as signs of God's active involvement in your weekly life.

# Step 4: Acknowledgment of Failures and Challenges

Reflect on the moments when you may have felt disconnected from God's presence or strayed from your values during the week. These instances are not meant for self-condemnation but for honest self-awareness and growth. Acknowledge them with compassion and a willingness to learn, recognizing that imperfection is an integral part of the human experience.

## Step 5: Resolution for the Coming Week

As you conclude the Weekly Examen, look ahead to the future with a heart filled with hope. Based on your reflections, set a simple intention or resolution for the week to come. This could be a commitment to be more attentive, a desire to express gratitude more frequently, or a willingness to seek guidance in challenging moments. Allow this resolution to be your guiding star as you continue your journey through the tapestry of life. There is a journaling section accompanying the Weekly Examen for you to write down your reflections and intentions.

Engaging in the Weekly Examen, you craft a space for divine illumination amidst the ebb and flow of your weekly existence. This practice encourages conscious and contemplative living, nurtures your relationship with God, and guides you toward a more intentional and meaningful weekly journey.

# Nurturing Reflection as a Family: Embracing the Weekly Examen Together

Bringing the transformative power of the Weekly Examen into your family life can cultivate deeper connections, nurture gratitude, and foster spiritual growth among both adults and children. This practice offers an opportunity to bond over shared reflections, celebrate moments of joy, and support one another through challenges.

Remember, adapting the Weekly Examen for children involves simplicity and creativity. Keep the language and concepts age-appropriate. Use stories, metaphors, or drawings to help children express their thoughts and feelings. By making this practice a part of your family routine, you nurture a sense of shared spirituality and cultivate a space where everyone feels seen, heard, and valued. Here's how you can integrate the Weekly Examen into your family routine:

## Step 1: Choose a Time:

Designate a consistent time each week for your family's Daily Examen. This could be before or after a meal, during bedtime, or any other time that suits your family's schedule. Consistency will help make the practice a cherished part of your daily life.

## Step 2: Create a Sacred Space

Find a quiet and comfortable space where your family can gather. Light a candle or place a small object as a symbol of the sacred. This can help set the tone for the reflective practice.

## Step 3: Gratitude Circle

Begin with a gratitude circle. Each family member takes turns sharing something they are thankful for from their day. This sets a positive and appreciative tone for the reflection.

## Step 4: Review of the Day

Guide your family through a review of the week's events. Ask questions like "What was the best part of your week?" or "Was there a moment that made you smile?" Encourage children to share about their activities, interactions, and feelings.

## Step 5: Recognition of Blessings

Prompt your family to recognize moments when they felt loved, supported, or inspired. Discuss these instances, allowing each family member to share their experiences. This encourages children to notice the positive influences in their lives.

## Step 6: Acknowledgment of Challenges

Create a safe space for family members, especially children, to discuss any difficulties they encountered during the day. Let them know that it's okay to share frustrations or struggles. This fosters open communication and empathy within the family.

## Step 7: Shared Intentions

As a family, set intentions for the following week. Ask questions like "How can we help each other this week?" or "What is something kind you can do for someone else?" Encourage children to come up with their own intentions and commitments.

## Step 8: Closing Prayer

Conclude the Weekly Examen with a brief prayer. Express gratitude for the week's blessings, ask for guidance, and offer support to each other. This can be as simple as holding hands and sharing a few heartfelt words.

# The Transformative Power of Journaling: Nurturing Self-Awareness and Divine Connection

In the sacred practice of Lectio Divina, journaling becomes a cherished companion, a vessel through which we navigate the depths of self-awareness and strengthen our bond with God. The act of translating the whispers of scripture and the echoes of our own hearts onto the pages of our journals is a profound act of mindfulness. It invites us to slow down, listen intently, and reflect deeply, cultivating a heightened self-awareness that forms the cornerstone of personal growth. Through the written word, we not only document our spiritual journey but also create a tangible record of our evolving relationship with God. As we pour our thoughts, insights, and prayers onto these pages, we forge a bridge between the human and the divine, fostering a connection that deepens with each stroke of the pen. The journal becomes a sacred space where our innermost thoughts and the wisdom of scripture converge, allowing us to witness our spiritual evolution and feel the ever-present embrace of the divine in the sanctuary of our own words.

Journaling pages are placed throughout your journal to provide space for this introspective chronicle of your journey. Whether it be a free flow of thoughts to paper, a verse re-written as a prayer, or a list of your worries that you would like to transfer to God as prayers, use these pages however you feel inspired at the moment.

# The Healing Art of Drawing: A Path to Inner Calm and Self-Discovery

In the realm of self-exploration and mindfulness, the soothing rhythm of a pen gliding across paper or the gentle strokes of a brush can be just as powerful as words. Meditative drawing, an exquisite fusion of artistic expression and contemplative practice, offers a sanctuary for those seeking tranquility, self-discovery, and a profound connection with their inner selves. Just as meditation can still the mind and unveil deeper truths, creating art mindfully can awaken dormant creativity, release emotional tension, and pave the way for profound revelations.

Modern life often runs at a frenetic pace and moments of quietude can be elusive. The mind often becomes a battleground of thoughts vying for attention. Here, meditative drawing steps in as a mindful refuge. Engaging in the deliberate act of drawing or painting, one stroke at a time, allows us to anchor our attention in the present moment. The gentle focus on shapes, lines, and colors becomes a form of active meditation, quieting the mental chatter and opening up a space for introspection. This process not only promotes relaxation but also encourages the emergence of unspoken emotions and hidden corners of the psyche.

Moreover, meditative drawing grants us a canvas to explore the landscapes of our thoughts and feelings without judgment. As we immerse ourselves in the artistic process, we tap into a primal mode of communication that bypasses the limitations of language. Unencumbered by the need for precision or representation, our art becomes a conduit for raw expression, enabling us to externalize our inner experiences in a non-threatening and liberating manner. In these strokes and shades, we often find reflections of our true selves, mirroring emotions, aspirations, and fears that may have remained unspoken. This journal invites you to embark on a dual journey – one of inner exploration and artistic creation – as you fuse the transformative powers of meditative drawing with the introspective journey of Lectio Divina. Let the colors and lines flow, as you rediscover yourself within the tapestry of your unique creations.

# Embracing the Uncharted: Cultivating Artistic Expression Beyond Fear

It's not uncommon for many to feel a sense of apprehension when faced with the prospect of drawing or painting, believing that artistry resides only in the hands of a select few. However, it's essential to recognize that artistic expression is not about adhering to predefined standards of beauty or perfection. Instead, it's a deeply personal journey of self-discovery and communication. The canvas, much like the pages of your meditation journal, is a space for authenticity, not for judgment. Art is not about being "good" at it; it's about allowing yourself to be vulnerable, to explore the uncharted territory of your creativity, and liberate your inner voice. With each stroke and color, you embark on a voyage of self-expression that transcends the fear of judgment. Embrace the blank page, for it is an open invitation to discover the artist within, and remember, there's no right or wrong in art—only the beautiful tapestry of your unique soul waiting to be unveiled.

# Guiding Your Creative Journey: Artistic Prompts and Coloring Pages

For those who may be hesitant or feel unsure about their artistic abilities, we're here to provide support every step of the way. Within the pages of this meditation journal, you'll find not only blank canvases but also carefully curated coloring pages and artistic prompts designed to kindle your creative spark. These resources are gentle guides, offering a helping hand as you navigate the world of meditative drawing. Allow them to be your companions, inspiring your artistic explorations and providing a sense of direction when you're unsure where to begin. Remember, there are no expectations here, only an invitation to discover the joy of self-expression and the tranquility that comes with letting your creativity flow freely. So, take a deep breath, pick up your colors, and let the artistry within you emerge, one stroke at a time.

# Serene Sketches:
## Finding Peace Through Meditative Sketching

We created Serene Sketches as a tranquil sanctuary, dedicated to calming the mind and imbuing everyday life with the soothing essence of art. This program is thoughtfully designed to unlock the therapeutic potential of meditative sketching, extending a heartfelt invitation to participants to embark on a transformative voyage of self-discovery and inner tranquility. Through the graceful union of repetitive patterns and mindful creativity, Serene Sketches seeks to guide individuals toward a profound sense of serenity and peace that can be seamlessly integrated into their everyday lives. As we explore the delicate dance of lines and shapes on paper, we unlock the artistic potential within us. We also open a doorway to inner serenity, enabling us to navigate the complexities of life with grace and poise. Join us in this artistic odyssey, where sketching becomes a path to find solace, balance, and a deep connection with the tranquil beauty residing within us all.

## Preparation

Begin by gathering your doodling supplies - a blank sheet of paper or a dedicated sketchbook, fine-tip markers or pens in various thicknesses, and a comfortable, quiet space. Take a few deep breaths to center yourself and set the intention for a meditative experience.

## Select Your Patterns

Choose three to four simple and repetitive patterns that resonate with you. These could include elements like waves, spirals, dots, or hatching lines. You can also create your patterns. The key is that they should be easy to draw repeatedly without much effort.

## Start with a Centerpiece

In the center of your paper, draw a small shape or design element. This will be your focal point. It can be a circle, a flower, a star, or anything that inspires you.

## Radiate Patterns

Begin by selecting one of your chosen patterns. Start drawing it outward from your centerpiece radially or concentrically. Let your hand move naturally, and don't worry about perfect symmetry. The goal is to create a sense of flow and repetition.

## Combine Patterns

As you continue to radiate your first pattern, feel free to introduce another pattern into the design. For example, if you started with waves, you can now add dots or spirals in between the waves. Let them interact and merge organically.

## Follow Your Intuition

Allow your intuition to guide you as you doodle. There's no right or wrong way to combine patterns. The process is about being present in the moment and letting your creativity flow without judgment.

## Repeat and Expand

Continue to expand your design, adding more patterns as you go along. Gradually fill the entire page or create a design that feels complete to you. This is a meditative journey, so take your time and enjoy the process. However, it should also be a relaxing process. So, if you ever feel pressured or frustrated, take a break and come back to it later.

## Color (Optional)

If you wish, you can add color to your Serene Sketches. Use colored markers, pencils, or watercolors to enhance the visual appeal of your creation.

## Embrace Enjoyment and Flexibility

Remember, the Serene Sketch process should be enjoyable and flexible. You can choose to work on a small portion of the paper or fill up the entire page—whatever feels right at the moment. Take as little or as much time as you desire; there's no rush. If at any point it begins to feel stressful or you find yourself striving for perfection, gently put it down. The essence of this practice lies in finding joy and relaxation through creativity, so let go of any expectations and allow your meditative sketch to flow organically.

## Reflect and Journal

After you've finished your doodle, take a moment to sit quietly and reflect on your experience. Consider how you felt during the process and any insights that arose. Journal your thoughts and feelings, as this can deepen your connection to the meditative practice.

## Repeat Regularly

To fully experience the benefits of meditative doodling with multiple patterns, make it a regular practice. Set aside time each day or week to explore new combinations and designs. Over time, you'll find that this creative practice not only brings tranquility but also enhances your artistic skills and inner awareness.

## Pattern Ideas

At the end of the journal, we've provided some pages of pattern ideas for you to use during your Serene Sketches process. You can use these to spur on your creative process in doodling. Some other ideas are to search patterns on the internet. We also love to search artists on Instagram and pinterest for fun ideas. Enjoy the process, have fun and just try different patterns together and see what ends up on the page!

"Good artists copy, great artists steal" - attributed to Pablo Picasso

# From Reflection to Action: Translating Lectio Divina Insights into Daily Practice

The journey of Lectio Divina is one of introspection and connection with our Father, but its true essence blooms when its revelations are woven into the fabric of everyday life. As you engage in the sacred process of divine reading and contemplation, consider the following prompts to help you translate the wisdom you've gained into meaningful actions that can inspire positive change in your daily interactions and the world around you.

## Volunteer

Embrace the spirit of compassion and service by volunteering your time and skills to a cause close to your heart. Reflect on the insights you've gained through Lectio Divina and find ways to apply them in your volunteer activities. Whether you decide to serve at your church, support a local charity, assist at a community event, or contribute to a social initiative, your actions can tangibly embody the values you've cultivated. Acts of service and compassion toward others are seen as acts of service to God Himself. Selfless giving and serving those in need reflect the values of compassion and empathy cultivated through practices like Lectio Divina.

**"Truly I tell you, whatever you did for one of the least of these brothers and sisters of mine, you did for me." Matthew 25:40 (NIV)**

## Give

Incorporate the practice of generosity into your routine by giving in ways that resonate with your inner reflections. This could be committing to tithe at your home church, donating to a charity aligned with your values, sharing your expertise to help someone in need, or simply offering a helping hand to a friend or neighbor. Ask God to open your eyes and heart to new ways to give. Let your actions mirror the abundance of insight and compassion you've nurtured through Lectio Divina. God encourages us to give with a joyful and willing heart; the act of giving should come from a place of sincere compassion and inner reflection.

**"Each of you should give what you have decided in your heart to give, not reluctantly or under compulsion, for God loves a cheerful giver." 2 Corinthians 9:7 (NIV)**

## Share What You've Learned

The insights you've uncovered during Lectio Divina hold the power to inspire others. Share your reflections, experiences, and the wisdom you've gained with friends, family, or online communities. Through this, you create a ripple effect, spreading the transformative energy of divine reading to others who may benefit from its impact.

**"As iron sharpens iron, so one person sharpens another." Proverbs 27:17 (NIV)**

## Connect with Friends

Oftentimes, we feel like in order to "do good in the world" we need to help strangers in need. However, more often than not, we have friends in our own close circle who are hurting silently and could use someone to reach out to them. Engage in heart-to-heart conversations with your friends, weaving the themes and insights from your Lectio Divina practice into your interactions. By sharing your reflections and inviting them to do the same, you create opportunities for mutual growth and deepen your connections. You may be the answer to your own friend's prayer.

**"Perfume and incense bring joy to the heart, and the pleasantness of a friend springs from their heartfelt advice." Proverbs 27:9 (NIV)**

## Connect with a Stranger

Broaden your sphere of connection to encompass individuals you may not typically engage with. Initiate a meaningful conversation with a stranger, whether it's a coworker, a neighbor, or someone you meet during your daily activities. By exchanging insights and attentively listening to their perspective, you nurture a profound sense of empathy and unity that transcends the boundaries of our differences.

**"Do not forget to show hospitality to strangers, for by so doing some people have shown hospitality to angels without knowing it." Hebrews 13:2 (NIV)**

## Inspire Someone

Let the wisdom you've gleaned from Lectio Divina be a source of inspiration for those around you. Whether through your actions, words, or creative expressions, aim to uplift and motivate someone in your life. By being a conduit of Jesus' love, you amplify the transformative impact of your contemplative journey.

**"Do nothing out of selfish ambition or vain conceit. Rather, in humility value others above yourselves, not looking to your own interests but each of you to the interests of the others." Philippians 2:3-4 (NIV)**

As you contemplate these prompts and take intentional steps to translate your Lectio Divina insights into actions, you infuse your daily life with the profound insights and spiritual growth that the practice offers. Each action becomes a testament to the deep connection between reflection, God's purpose for you, and tangible change, shaping a more conscious and compassionate way of living.

# Elevating Your Lectio Divina Journey: Exploring Group Practice and the Power of Essential Oils

As you embark on your journey of Lectio Divina, two enriching avenues can enhance your contemplative experience. First, the practice of group Lectio Divina offers a communal embrace of the sacred text, fostering collective insight and shared spiritual growth. In the presence of fellow seekers, the wisdom of Scripture takes on new dimensions. Sharing your thoughts with a group can deepen your connection with God and those who share in your quest for spiritual understanding. Additionally, incorporating essential oils, known for their evocative scents and therapeutic properties, can elevate your contemplative environment. Essential oils can help you attain a heightened state of mindfulness and serenity. These two optional elements are powerful tools that can help you draw closer to the profound wisdom held within the Bible.

## The Collective Harmony of Group Lectio Divina: Uniting Hearts and Minds

Embarking on the journey of Lectio Divina within a group setting adds a dimension of shared experience and collective growth that enhances the practice's profound benefits. Here are some compelling reasons why practicing Lectio Divina in a group can be transformative:

### Shared Wisdom and Insights

Group sessions of Lectio Divina create an environment where diverse perspectives converge. As each participant shares their insights and reflections, a tapestry of interpretations unfolds. This collective wisdom offers new angles and meanings to the chosen text, expanding everyone's understanding and enriching the experience.

## Amplified Presence

In a group, the energy and intention of each participant contribute to a heightened sense of presence. As you sit together, the combined focus on the Scriptures generates a palpable atmosphere of reverence. This shared concentration magnifies the impact of the practice, fostering a deeper connection with the Word of God and the Holy Spirit.

## Mutual Support and Encouragement

Group sessions provide a network of support that can be particularly encouraging during challenging times. Sharing personal reflections and insights with others fosters an atmosphere of trust and empathy, where individuals feel seen and heard. This mutual exchange of vulnerability strengthens the bonds of community and reinforces the practice's value.

## Accountability and Consistency

The commitment to attending group sessions encourages consistency in the practice. Knowing that others are growing in their faith by practicing Lectio Divina can motivate individuals to prioritize this time for themselves. This accountability nurtures a sense of dedication and helps overcome obstacles that might otherwise deter personal practice.

## Deeper Exploration

The group dynamic often prompts participants to explore facets of the text that they might not have considered on their own. Engaging in open discussions and listening to different interpretations fosters an atmosphere of inquiry and curiosity, leading to a deeper exploration of the chosen scripture.

## Spiritual Fellowship

Group Lectio Divina is not just a practice; it's an opportunity for spiritual fellowship. Participants share in a collective journey of self-discovery and connection with God. This shared experience can lead to lasting friendships and a sense of belonging that extends beyond the sessions themselves.

In essence, practicing Lectio Divina in a group setting elevates the experience from a personal contemplation to a communal exploration. The collective energy, shared insights, and mutual support create a dynamic synergy that deepens your connection with the sacred, enriches your understanding of the text, and fosters a sense of unity among participants. As you gather in a circle of shared intention, you embark on a transformative journey that transcends individual boundaries, nurturing the growth of mind, heart, and spirit. Consider practicing Lectio Divina with your church small group, youth group, or just your group of friends.

# Elevating the Senses: Deepening the Lectio Divina Experience with Essential Oils

The power of scent can be used as a portal to enhanced contemplation and heightened presence. Introducing essential oils into your Lectio Divina practice can magnify the sensory journey, creating an immersive environment that aligns your mind, body, and spirit. Just as passages of Scripture evoke profound emotions, the aroma of essential oils can evoke memories, emotions, and states of being that resonate with the essence of your chosen practice. The intricate dance of scent and spirituality offers a harmonious symphony that deepens your connection to the divine, transforming your practice of Lectio Divina into an all-encompassing sensory voyage. You can diffuse essential oils or add a few drops to your hand, rub your hands together, and then inhale a few deep breaths while cupping your hands near your nose. We recommend using just one oil or one blend during a session of Lectio Divina. To incorporate essential oils, simply inhale the scent before you begin.

Some of our favorite essential oils to incorporate into prayer, meditation, and Lectio Divina are:

- Palo Santo
- Frankincense
- Sandalwood
- Ylang Ylang
- Bergamot
- Clary Sage
- Lavender
- Myrhh
- Neroli
- Cedarwood
- Sage
- Vetiver

# Carving Out Sacred Time Amidst the Bustle: Incorporating Daily Lectio Divina

In the whirlwind of our hectic lives, it's crucial to intentionally create pockets of time dedicated to deepening our relationship with our Creator. The sacred practice of Lectio Divina can be a powerful complement to your spiritual rituals or even a great way to begin establishing a consistent routine of connecting with God. Begin by identifying windows in your daily routine to accommodate this meaningful contemplation. Whether you wake up a few minutes earlier, set aside moments during a lunch break, or incorporate it into your evening wind-down ritual, prioritizing Lectio Divina is akin to setting aside a precious appointment with your soul. Dedicate this time with intention and steadfastness, gradually weaving it into the fabric of your daily life. By doing so, you invite the transformative power of divine reading to infuse your days with moments of tranquility, reflection, and spiritual growth, enriching your connection with the sacred amidst life's busy rhythms.

## Creating a Sacred Space

While finding a serene retreat might seem challenging, even a small corner can become a sacred space for your practice. Arrange a few meaningful objects, like a candle, a cushion, and your Bible, to infuse the space with intention. Creating this space communicates to your subconscious that you are entering a realm of contemplation and mindfulness. Over time, this space becomes a haven where you can connect with yourself and the divine, no matter how brief the moment.

## Steadfast and Persevering

Adopting the Lectio Divina into your routine is a commitment to personal and spiritual growth. However, there may be days when busyness and distractions make it challenging to engage fully. During such times, remind yourself that the essence of the practice lies not in perfection, but in the sincere effort to show up for yourself and your well-being. Allow flexibility in the timing or adapt the practice as needed. The key is approaching it with a resilient heart, knowing that each effort contributes to your overall journey.

# Having Grace for Yourself When It Doesn't Go as Planned

Life is unpredictable, and there will be days when your intention to practice Lectio Divina might be interrupted or forgotten altogether. It's crucial to approach these moments with self-compassion and grace. Instead of self-judgment, acknowledge the circumstances that led to the disruption and gently recommit to the practice the following day. Remember that this journey is about progress, not perfection. By embracing these lapses without self-criticism, you will find it easier to pick the practice back up and continue your journey to a deeper relationship with your Creator.

As you weave Lectio Divina into the tapestry of your busy life, recognize that each stride you take towards mindfulness and self-awareness reflects your unwavering commitment to personal well-being and spiritual connection. Through incremental adjustments, the nurturing of a sacred sanctuary, persistent engagement, and the generous gift of grace to yourself, you construct a resilient framework for this practice to thrive amid the hustle and clamor of your daily existence.

# Embarking on Your Transformative Journey

As you stand at the threshold of this transformative journey through Lectio Divina, we extend to you a heartfelt welcome. This practice is a profound voyage of self-discovery, spiritual connection, and growth. We invite you not only to embark on this journey but also to share your insights, experiences, and the beauty you uncover along the way with our vibrant community on our social media pages. In doing so, you contribute to the collective tapestry of wisdom and inspire others on their paths of contemplation and spiritual awakening. Together, we forge a sacred space for reflection, growth, and the celebration of the divine within and around us. So, with an open heart and a curious spirit, let us begin this incredible expedition, ready to unveil the treasures that Lectio Divina holds for each of us.

# Quietude

Date:___/___/____

Prepare for today's sacred reading with a few moments of quieting the mind and soul

# Lectio  Isaiah 40:8

Read the Scripture out loud slowly, listening & creating space for the words. Repeat up to 3x.

# Meditatio

Choose a word, phrase, or concept that speaks to you and write these down.

_____

_____

_____

_____

_____

# Oratio

Respond to the insights God has shown you as a prayer, journaling, or conversation with God.

_____

_____

_____

_____

_____

# Contemplatio

Rest in God's love, allowing the echoes of the reading, reflection, and response to settle within you.

# Quietude

Date:___/___/____

Prepare for today's sacred reading with a few moments of quieting the mind and soul

# Lectio *Ephesians 3:14-19*

Read the Scripture out loud slowly, listening & creating space for the words. Repeat up to 3x.

# Meditatio

Choose a word, phrase, or concept that speaks to you and write these down.

_____

_____

_____

_____

_____

# Oratio

Respond to the insights God has shown you as a prayer, journaling, or conversation with God.

_____

_____

_____

_____

_____

# Contemplatio

Rest in God's love, allowing the echoes of the reading, reflection, and response to settle within you.

# Art

Create a visual representation of something that you learned from today's Lectio Divina.

OR

Select a prompt from the Artistic Prompts section located at the end of the journal.

OR

Create your own Serene Sketch.

# Quietude

Date:__/__/___

Prepare for today's sacred reading with a few moments of quieting the mind and soul

# Lectio   Philippians 1:3-6

Read the Scripture out loud slowly, listening & creating space for the words. Repeat up to 3x.

# Meditatio

Choose a word, phrase, or concept that speaks to you and write these down.

_____

_____

_____

_____

_____

# Oratio

Respond to the insights God has shown you as a prayer, journaling, or conversation with God.

_____

_____

_____

_____

_____

# Contemplatio

Rest in God's love, allowing the echoes of the reading, reflection, and response to settle within you.

# Quietude

Date:___/___/___

Prepare for today's sacred reading with a few moments of quieting the mind and soul

# Lectio  Colossians 3:1-4

Read the Scripture out loud slowly, listening & creating space for the words. Repeat up to 3x.

# Meditatio

Choose a word, phrase, or concept that speaks to you and write these down.

_____

_____

_____

_____

_____

# Oratio

Respond to the insights God has shown you as a prayer, journaling, or conversation with God.

_____

_____

_____

_____

_____

# Contemplatio

Rest in God's love, allowing the echoes of the reading, reflection, and response to settle within you.

# Art

Create a visual representation of something that you learned from today's Lectio Divina.

OR

Select a prompt from the Artistic Prompts section located at the end of the journal.

OR

Create your own Serene Sketch.

# Quietude

Date:__/__/____

Prepare for today's sacred reading with a few moments of quieting the mind and soul

# Lectio  2 Thessalonians 1:3-5

Read the Scripture out loud slowly, listening & creating space for the words. Repeat up to 3x.

# Meditatio

Choose a word, phrase, or concept that speaks to you and write these down.

_____

_____

_____

_____

_____

_____

_____

# Oratio

Respond to the insights God has shown you as a prayer, journaling, or conversation with God.

_____

_____

_____

_____

_____

# Contemplatio

Rest in God's love, allowing the echoes of the reading, reflection, and response to settle within you.

# Weekly Examen Prayer

Date:___/___/____

## Step 1: Gratitude for God's Presence

As you close your eyes and take a few deep breaths, think about the past week. What are you most grateful for in terms of God's presence and guidance in your life during this time?

## Step 2: Review of the Week

Begin to mentally revisit the week, starting from its beginning. What were the significant moments or experiences that stand out to you, and why do they hold significance? Reflect on how these moments aligned with your inner values.

## Step 3: Recognition of God's Presence

Recall moments during the week when you felt a strong sense of God's presence or guidance. Were there any particular instances that brought you joy, inspiration, or a connection to God? Describe these moments and their impact on you.

## Step 4: Acknowledgment of Failures and Challenges

Consider times when you may have felt disconnected from God or faced challenges in living out your values. Without judgment, recognize these moments and reflect on what you can learn from them. How can you grow through acknowledging imperfection?

## Step 5: Resolution for the Coming Week

Looking forward to the week ahead, what simple intention or resolution can you set based on your reflections from this Weekly Examen? How do you aspire to deepen your connection with God and align with your values in the coming days?

_____

_____

_____

_____

# Weekly Examen Prayer

# Journal

# Quietude

Date:___/___/_____

Prepare for today's sacred reading with a few moments of quieting the mind and soul

# Lectio   Psalm 73: 21-28

Read the Scripture out loud slowly, listening & creating space for the words. Repeat up to 3x.

# Meditatio

Choose a word, phrase, or concept that speaks to you and write these down.

_____

_____

_____

_____

_____

# Oratio

Respond to the insights God has shown you as a prayer, journaling, or conversation with God.

_____

_____

_____

_____

_____

# Contemplatio

Rest in God's love, allowing the echoes of the reading, reflection, and response to settle within you.

# Art

Create a visual representation of something that you learned from today's Lectio Divina.

OR

Select a prompt from the Artistic Prompts section located at the end of the journal.

OR

Create your own Serene Sketch.

# Quietude

Date:___/___/___

Prepare for today's sacred reading with a few moments of quieting the mind and soul

# Lectio Colossians 3:12-15

Read the Scripture out loud slowly, listening & creating space for the words. Repeat up to 3x.

# Meditatio

Choose a word, phrase, or concept that speaks to you and write these down.

_____

_____

_____

_____

_____

# Oratio

Respond to the insights God has shown you as a prayer, journaling, or conversation with God.

_____

_____

_____

_____

_____

# Contemplatio

Rest in God's love, allowing the echoes of the reading, reflection, and response to settle within you.

# Quietude

Prepare for today's sacred reading with a few moments of quieting the mind and soul

# Lectio 2 Timothy 1:5-7

Read the Scripture out loud slowly, listening & creating space for the words. Repeat up to 3x.

# Meditatio

Choose a word, phrase, or concept that speaks to you and write these down.

_____

_____

_____

_____

_____

# Oratio

Respond to the insights God has shown you as a prayer, journaling, or conversation with God.

_____

_____

_____

_____

_____

# Contemplatio

Rest in God's love, allowing the echoes of the reading, reflection, and response to settle within you.

# Art

Create a visual representation of something that you learned from today's Lectio Divina.

OR

Select a prompt from the Artistic Prompts section located at the end of the journal.

OR

Create your own Serene Sketch.

# Quietude

Date: __/__/___

Prepare for today's sacred reading with a few moments of quieting the mind and soul

# Lectio  James 3:17-18

Read the Scripture out loud slowly, listening & creating space for the words. Repeat up to 3x.

# Meditatio

Choose a word, phrase, or concept that speaks to you and write these down.

_____

_____

_____

_____

_____

# Oratio

Respond to the insights God has shown you as a prayer, journaling, or conversation with God.

_____

_____

_____

_____

_____

# Contemplatio

Rest in God's love, allowing the echoes of the reading, reflection, and response to settle within you.

# Quietude

Prepare for today's sacred reading with a few moments of quieting the mind and soul

# Lectio *Psalm 31:1-5*

Read the Scripture out loud slowly, listening & creating space for the words. Repeat up to 3x.

# Meditatio

Choose a word, phrase, or concept that speaks to you and write these down.

_____

_____

_____

_____

_____

_____

# Oratio

Respond to the insights God has shown you as a prayer, journaling, or conversation with God.

_____

_____

_____

_____

_____

# Contemplatio

Rest in God's love, allowing the echoes of the reading, reflection, and response to settle within you.

# Art

Create a visual representation of something that you learned from today's Lectio Divina.

OR

Select a prompt from the Artistic Prompts section located at the end of the journal.

OR

Create your own Serene Sketch.

# Weekly Examen Prayer

Date:___/___/____

## Step 1: Gratitude for God's Presence

As you close your eyes and take a few deep breaths, think about the past week. What are you most grateful for in terms of God's presence and guidance in your life during this time?

## Step 2: Review of the Week

Begin to mentally revisit the week, starting from its beginning. What were the significant moments or experiences that stand out to you, and why do they hold significance? Reflect on how these moments aligned with your inner values.

## Step 3: Recognition of God's Presence

Recall moments during the week when you felt a strong sense of God's presence or guidance. Were there any particular instances that brought you joy, inspiration, or a connection to God? Describe these moments and their impact on you.

## Step 4: Acknowledgment of Failures and Challenges

Consider times when you may have felt disconnected from God or faced challenges in living out your values. Without judgment, recognize these moments and reflect on what you can learn from them. How can you grow through acknowledging imperfection?

## Step 5: Resolution for the Coming Week

Looking forward to the week ahead, what simple intention or resolution can you set based on your reflections from this Weekly Examen? How do you aspire to deepen your connection with God and align with your values in the coming days?

_____

_____

_____

_____

# Weekly Examen Prayer

# Journal

# Quietude

Prepare for today's sacred reading with a few moments of quieting the mind and soul

# Lectio    Ephesians 4:30-32

Read the Scripture out loud slowly, listening & creating space for the words. Repeat up to 3x.

# Meditatio

Choose a word, phrase, or concept that speaks to you and write these down.

_____

_____

_____

_____

_____

_____

# Oratio

Respond to the insights God has shown you as a prayer, journaling, or conversation with God.

_____

_____

_____

_____

_____

# Contemplatio

Rest in God's love, allowing the echoes of the reading, reflection, and response to settle within you.

# Quietude

Date:___/___/____

Prepare for today's sacred reading with a few moments of quieting the mind and soul

# Lectio  *Proverbs 18:17-21*

Read the Scripture out loud slowly, listening & creating space for the words. Repeat up to 3x.

# Meditatio

Choose a word, phrase, or concept that speaks to you and write these down.

_____

_____

_____

_____

_____

_____

# Oratio

Respond to the insights God has shown you as a prayer, journaling, or conversation with God.

_____

_____

_____

_____

_____

# Contemplatio

Rest in God's love, allowing the echoes of the reading, reflection, and response to settle within you.

# Art

Create a visual representation of something that you learned from today's Lectio Divina.

OR

Select a prompt from the Artistic Prompts section located at the end of the journal.

OR

Create your own Serene Sketch.

# Quietude

Prepare for today's sacred reading with a few moments of quieting the mind and soul

# Lectio *Romans 1:16-17*

Read the Scripture out loud slowly, listening & creating space for the words. Repeat up to 3x.

# Meditatio

Choose a word, phrase, or concept that speaks to you and write these down.

_____

_____

_____

_____

_____

_____

# Oratio

Respond to the insights God has shown you as a prayer, journaling, or conversation with God.

_____

_____

_____

_____

_____

# Contemplatio

Rest in God's love, allowing the echoes of the reading, reflection, and response to settle within you.

# Quietude

Date:___/___/_____

Prepare for today's sacred reading with a few moments of quieting the mind and soul

# Lectio   *James 1:16-18*

Read the Scripture out loud slowly, listening & creating space for the words. Repeat up to 3x.

# Meditatio

Choose a word, phrase, or concept that speaks to you and write these down.

_____

_____

_____

_____

_____

# Oratio

Respond to the insights God has shown you as a prayer, journaling, or conversation with God.

_____

_____

_____

_____

_____

# Contemplatio

Rest in God's love, allowing the echoes of the reading, reflection, and response to settle within you.

# Art

Create a visual representation of something that you learned from today's Lectio Divina.

OR

Select a prompt from the Artistic Prompts section located at the end of the journal.

OR

Create your own Serene Sketch.

# Quietude

Date:___/___/___

Prepare for today's sacred reading with a few moments of quieting the mind and soul

# Lectio  Psalm 39:4-7

Read the Scripture out loud slowly, listening & creating space for the words. Repeat up to 3x.

# Meditatio

Choose a word, phrase, or concept that speaks to you and write these down.

_____

_____

_____

_____

_____

# Oratio

Respond to the insights God has shown you as a prayer, journaling, or conversation with God.

_____

_____

_____

_____

_____

# Contemplatio

Rest in God's love, allowing the echoes of the reading, reflection, and response to settle within you.

# Weekly Examen Prayer

Date:___/___/____

## Step 1: Gratitude for God's Presence

As you close your eyes and take a few deep breaths, think about the past week. What are you most grateful for in terms of God's presence and guidance in your life during this time?

## Step 2: Review of the Week

Begin to mentally revisit the week, starting from its beginning. What were the significant moments or experiences that stand out to you, and why do they hold significance? Reflect on how these moments aligned with your inner values.

## Step 3: Recognition of God's Presence

Recall moments during the week when you felt a strong sense of God's presence or guidance. Were there any particular instances that brought you joy, inspiration, or a connection to God? Describe these moments and their impact on you.

## Step 4: Acknowledgment of Failures and Challenges

Consider times when you may have felt disconnected from God or faced challenges in living out your values. Without judgment, recognize these moments and reflect on what you can learn from them. How can you grow through acknowledging imperfection?

## Step 5: Resolution for the Coming Week

Looking forward to the week ahead, what simple intention or resolution can you set based on your reflections from this Weekly Examen? How do you aspire to deepen your connection with God and align with your values in the coming days?

_____

_____

_____

_____

# Weekly Examen Prayer

# Journal

# Quietude

Prepare for today's sacred reading with a few moments of quieting the mind and soul

# Lectio  *Deuteronomy 30:11-16*

Read the Scripture out loud slowly, listening & creating space for the words. Repeat up to 3x.

# Meditatio

Choose a word, phrase, or concept that speaks to you and write these down.

_____

_____

_____

_____

_____

_____

# Oratio

Respond to the insights God has shown you as a prayer, journaling, or conversation with God.

_____

_____

_____

_____

_____

# Contemplatio

Rest in God's love, allowing the echoes of the reading, reflection, and response to settle within you.

# Art

Create a visual representation of something that you learned from today's Lectio Divina.

OR

Select a prompt from the Artistic Prompts section located at the end of the journal.

OR

Create your own Serene Sketch.

# Quietude

Date:___/___/____

Prepare for today's sacred reading with a few moments of quieting the mind and soul

# Lectio  *Ephesians 3:20-21*

Read the Scripture out loud slowly, listening & creating space for the words. Repeat up to 3x.

# Meditatio

Choose a word, phrase, or concept that speaks to you and write these down.

_____

_____

_____

_____

_____

# Oratio

Respond to the insights God has shown you as a prayer, journaling, or conversation with God.

_____

_____

_____

_____

# Contemplatio

Rest in God's love, allowing the echoes of the reading, reflection, and response to settle within you.

# Quietude

Prepare for today's sacred reading with a few moments of quieting the mind and soul

# Lectio  *Joshua 1:6-9*

Read the Scripture out loud slowly, listening & creating space for the words. Repeat up to 3x.

# Meditatio

Choose a word, phrase, or concept that speaks to you and write these down.

_____

_____

_____

_____

_____

# Oratio

Respond to the insights God has shown you as a prayer, journaling, or conversation with God.

_____

_____

_____

_____

_____

# Contemplatio

Rest in God's love, allowing the echoes of the reading, reflection, and response to settle within you.

# Art

Create a visual representation of something that you learned from today's Lectio Divina.

OR

Select a prompt from the Artistic Prompts section located at the end of the journal.

OR

Create your own Serene Sketch.

# Quietude

Date: ___/___/___

Prepare for today's sacred reading with a few moments of quieting the mind and soul

# Lectio  John 14:15-19

Read the Scripture out loud slowly, listening & creating space for the words. Repeat up to 3x.

# Meditatio

Choose a word, phrase, or concept that speaks to you and write these down.

_____

_____

_____

_____

_____

# Oratio

Respond to the insights God has shown you as a prayer, journaling, or conversation with God.

_____

_____

_____

_____

_____

# Contemplatio

Rest in God's love, allowing the echoes of the reading, reflection, and response to settle within you.

# Quietude

Date:___/___/___

Prepare for today's sacred reading with a few moments of quieting the mind and soul

# Lectio   Psalm 4:20-27

Read the Scripture out loud slowly, listening & creating space for the words. Repeat up to 3x.

# Meditatio

Choose a word, phrase, or concept that speaks to you and write these down.

_____

_____

_____

_____

_____

# Oratio

Respond to the insights God has shown you as a prayer, journaling, or conversation with God.

_____

_____

_____

_____

_____

# Contemplatio

Rest in God's love, allowing the echoes of the reading, reflection, and response to settle within you.

# Art

Create a visual representation of something that you learned from today's Lectio Divina.

OR

Select a prompt from the Artistic Prompts section located at the end of the journal.

OR

Create your own Serene Sketch.

# Weekly Examen Prayer

Date:___/___/___

## Step 1: Gratitude for God's Presence

As you close your eyes and take a few deep breaths, think about the past week. What are you most grateful for in terms of God's presence and guidance in your life during this time?

## Step 2: Review of the Week

Begin to mentally revisit the week, starting from its beginning. What were the significant moments or experiences that stand out to you, and why do they hold significance? Reflect on how these moments aligned with your inner values.

## Step 3: Recognition of God's Presence

Recall moments during the week when you felt a strong sense of God's presence or guidance. Were there any particular instances that brought you joy, inspiration, or a connection to God? Describe these moments and their impact on you.

## Step 4: Acknowledgment of Failures and Challenges

Consider times when you may have felt disconnected from God or faced challenges in living out your values. Without judgment, recognize these moments and reflect on what you can learn from them. How can you grow through acknowledging imperfection?

## Step 5: Resolution for the Coming Week

Looking forward to the week ahead, what simple intention or resolution can you set based on your reflections from this Weekly Examen? How do you aspire to deepen your connection with God and align with your values in the coming days?

_____

_____

_____

_____

# Weekly Examen Prayer

# Journal

# Monthly Reflection

As each month unfolds on your transformative journey through Lectio Divina, taking time for reflection becomes a vital part of your spiritual growth. This monthly review invites you to pause and ponder the depths of your contemplative exploration. Consider the words and scriptures that have graced your path and how they've resonated with your life's experiences, challenges, and joys. As you review your journal entries and meditative moments, you may find it beneficial to ask yourself a few guiding questions:

1. What Stood Out Most: Reflect on the scriptures or passages that stood out the most this month. Why did they resonate with you?

2. Did You Notice a Theme: Were there recurring themes or messages that emerged during your practice? How did they relate to your life circumstances?

3. What Did God Teach You: Explore the insights and wisdom you've gained during your Lectio Divina practice. What lessons has God revealed to you through these sacred words?

4. How Did You Grow: In what ways have you grown spiritually or emotionally during this month's journey?

5. Intentions for the Future: Based on your reflections, what intentions or aspirations do you have for the month ahead in your continued exploration of Lectio Divina?

This monthly review serves as an invaluable tool for tracking your progress, deepening your connection with the divine, and nurturing a more profound understanding of the sacred words that guide your path.

_____

_____

_____

_____

_____

_____

# Monthly Reflection

# From Reflection to Action:

## Translating Lectio Divina Insights into Daily Practice

It is time to implement what you've learned into active steps. Review the "Reflection to Action" prompts to begin to translate the wisdom you've gained into meaningful actions that can inspire positive change in your daily interactions and the world around you.

- ☐ Volunteer
- ☐ Give
- ☐ Share what you've learned
- ☐ Connect with friends
- ☐ Connect with a stranger
- ☐ Inspire someone

- Consider committing to a way to implement one of these into your life
- Brainstorm ideas of how you will put this into action
- List names of friends with whom you want to share what you've learned
- Once you've taken action, journal about the experience

_____

_____

_____

_____

_____

_____

_____

_____

_____

_____

# Artistic Prompts

# Artistic Prompts

Select one of these prompts to inspire your meditative art:

1. **Nature's Symphony:** Create a visual representation of the sounds of nature that soothe your soul during meditation.

2. **Sacred Symbols:** Illustrate a symbol or image that holds deep spiritual significance for you and write about its meaning.

3. **Dreamscape:** Sketch or paint a scene from a recent dream and explore its symbolism in your journal.

4. **Color Affirmations:** Choose a color that resonates with your current emotions and fill a page with it, then journal about the feelings it evokes.

5. **Soul Portrait:** Draw a self-portrait without focusing on physical features, but instead on representing your inner self.

6. **Mandalas:** Create intricate mandala patterns with colors and shapes that reflect your current emotional state.

7. **Path of Reflection:** Draw a winding path on your page and add symbols or images that represent your life's journey. Journal about what you discover along the way.

8. **Tree of Life:** Sketch a tree and its branches, using each branch to represent different aspects of your life. Write about what each branch signifies.

9. **Waves of Emotion:** Paint or draw a series of waves to represent your emotional highs and lows. Journal about what's causing these fluctuations.

10. **Vision Board:** Create a collage using images and words from magazines or printouts that represent your aspirations, dreams, and intentions.

# Artistic Prompts

Select 2-4 patterns to create your own meditative artwork piece:

# Artistic Prompts

Select 2-4 patterns to create your own meditative artwork piece:

# Artistic Prompts

Select 2-4 patterns to create your own meditative artwork piece:

# Artistic Prompts

Select 2-4 patterns to create your own meditative artwork piece:

# Artistic Prompts

Select 2-4 patterns to create your own meditative artwork piece:

# A Heartfelt Thank You

As you reach the end of this meditative journey, I want to extend my sincere gratitude to you. Thank you for embracing the call to try something new, for taking that courageous step toward deepening your relationship with God, and for placing your trust in me to guide you along this path. I am so grateful for your openness, curiosity, and commitment to this transformative experience. I hope that you've found solace, inspiration, and profound connection in these pages. Remember, your journey is a sacred and unique one. As you continue to explore and nurture your spiritual growth, may the peace, love, and wisdom you've discovered here accompany you on every step of your beautiful journey ahead.

♡ Samara

# Ways to Connect

Join our FB group for community support, Serene Sketches videos, and additional artistic prompts.
Still Waters & Abiding Peace

Share your Lectio Divina Journey and Tag us:
Still Waters & Abiding Peace
@SW.and.AP

# Devo with your Kids

For those who would like to share the Lectio Divina practice with your children, we've created a companion kids journal. This journal teaches your children the beautiful process of connecting with Scripture and listening to the Holy Spirit so that you can enjoy the process together.

Check out our FB Group and IG pages for more info on how to get the kids journal for your family.

Made in the USA
Las Vegas, NV
11 February 2024

85670119R00052